MARCO
MADE
EASY

★ ★ ★

This book is dedicated to Mirabelle,
the most beautiful girl in the world

MARCO MADE EASY

A Three-Star Chef Makes It Simple

MARCO PIERRE WHITE

WEIDENFELD & NICOLSON

This book was put together in my restaurant at Chelsea FC's Stamford Bridge ground. Some days I'd come in and think, we've got steak – let's see what we can do with it.

But it wasn't a solo journey: I was joined by others along the way. My assistant Mr Ishii got me there and back in the Range Rover, so I'll thank him first. And sincere thanks are due to my agent Jonathan Lloyd, of Curtis Brown. I am indebted to my kitchen vice-chairman Matt 'Bisto Boy' Brown for his invaluable assistance. And thank you Roger 'Rocket Man' Pizey, who aided and abetted when it came to desserts. Matt and Roger have been with me for 20 years; loyal shipmates they are. Julita Goralczuk was supportive and kept things sweet with tea and coffee.

Thanks are also due to Jill Mead, who photographed the dishes beautifully (and tried to make me laugh). Her assistant Mickey White kept track of the shots, so well done Mickey. Alex Smith of Smith & Gilmour designed the pages, and don't they look stunning?

Thank you to all at Weidenfeld & Nicolson, including Lucie Stericker and Nicki Crossley and, in particular, Michael Dover. Michael always retained faith in this project and will now (I hope) concede that patience is indeed a virtue.

My favourite co-author James Steen came into the kitchen with his laptop, ate all the food, wrote up the recipes, drank the wine, got a free cookery lesson, banked the cheque and nodded when I told him I couldn't have done it without him. Thank you James.

Contents

BEFORE you reach for the chopping board…

I've got a pub in Berkshire and like to head there when life in London becomes chaotic. Actually, the Yew Tree – with its Inglenook fireplace and cosy, warm dining room – is my favourite place in the world, though after a drop of Old Rosie cider you need to watch out for the low-beamed ceiling.

I was there the other night when a man came up to me and asked if I'd buy him a drink. 'Sir,' I said, 'the only thing on the house is the roof.' He laughed so, of course, I pulled him a pint.

And I was at the Yew Tree when I was presented with a dish that inspired this book. It was steak tartare, that dish of minced raw beef. As I stared at the plate it struck me that except for the steak and the raw egg yolk on top of it, most of the other ingredients came straight out of bottles. Tomato ketchup, mayonnaise, mustard, Worcestershire sauce and Tabasco – they all bring flavour to the dish and they are probably in your store-cupboard.

As I ate, I thought it might be a good idea to do a cookery book in which the main ingredient is not messed around with, but rather celebrated and shown off.

Too often cookery books try too hard and therefore they make the reader try too hard. I just don't get it. Life is complicated enough without introducing stress into the kitchen.

I like to keep things simple, and this book is all about creating beautiful and delicious food without any aggro. It's about producing big flavours, and the beauty of it all is that more often than not, no kitchen skill is required. You don't, for instance, need to be an artist to fold sea bass in tin foil. Equally,

the moules marinière and the peppered steak are two dishes that, when done well, will win smiles at any table in the land, but will not make the cook sweat.

This book is for anyone who loves food. The accomplished gourmet will appreciate the desire to show off the primary ingredient of a dish. The aspiring beginner or infrequent cook, on the other hand, can take comfort that most of the recipes need little know-how and little time.

In fact, it will take you longer to wash the dishes than it will to cook them.

The most commonly used phrase within these pages is 'to your taste'. In other words, taste, taste and taste – food that is perfect for you and your tastebuds.

Regularly I come across people who say they are frightened of cooking – they think they will mess it up, make a mistake. It is not just the aspiring home cook who suffers a fear of the stove. I've seen it in professional kitchens; those moments when a chef is petrified of taking centre stage at the hob. I really hope that these pages will instill confidence and dissolve the fear of the stove.

In *White Heat*, my first cookery book (it was published in 1990), I wrote, 'I can't work in a domestic kitchen; it's just too confined. There's no freedom and there's no buzz. At home I'm not hit with forty covers in half an hour so there's no real excitement.'

I've had to reassess my views after retiring from the professional kitchen more than a decade ago. Whether at home or in a restaurant, cooking has always been a way of life for me (I fell in love with it because it was the only way in which I could express myself). Cooking for guests in a restaurant is a tough job: the days are long and the nights are short. However, cooking for family and friends at home can't work if it is not a pleasurable experience. It has to be fun, and I hope that the ease of the recipes in this book will make you want to spend more time in the kitchen creating lovely meals. At home these days I am not hit with forty covers, but there is certainly a buzz to be had from making meals and I have long since discovered the freedom of my kitchen at home. (I have discovered the joys of shopping, too. I have to say, I love a shelf, I love a bottle and I love an aisle. That's why I got married three times.)

And on the subject of freedom, please use my recipes as a guide only. Don't feel restricted. Add or delete ingredients, as you see fit. Amend measurements, quantities and cooking times to suit your palate and your oven.

I declare an interest or two – I work with Knorr and within these pages I use Knorr's A Touch of Taste and their stock cubes. I use them because they add flavour and I treat them as a seasoning. If you disapprove don't use them. Likewise, I work with Bernard Matthews and in this book you will find turkey recipes. I love turkey and when cooked well – rather than dry – it is superior to most poultry.

I come from a background of training in classical French cuisine. As I worked my way up the ladder in the '70s and early '80s I was privileged to be mentored by the some of the greats, and it follows that many of the dishes that I have made over the years have been complex and required exceptional skill and knowledge in cooking techniques.

Here, I have used that skill, knowledge and experience to come up with recipes

that are fool-proof – but I have also tried to provide recipes for that dish which will create a sense of occasion that is vital for the Saturday night dinner party or Sunday lunch gathering. Also, each dish is photographed so that, if you like, you can copy my presentation.

But remember when cooking that all great chefs have three things in common. First, they accept and respect that Mother Nature is the true artist and that they are the cook. Second, everything they do is an extension of themselves. And third, they give you insight into the world they were born into, the world that inspired them, and they serve it on their plates.

A few minor points... When recipes refer to olive oil that'll be extra virgin olive oil; I also use clarified butter (or ghee) because I like it, but by all means use your favourite butter or an oil if you prefer. Salted or unsalted butter? Always unsalted – then you can add salt to your taste. When I refer to 'garnish' I am not thinking merely of decoration but also of ingredients that can be eaten, and be generous with it. When I talk of shrimps in the Shellfish section it is because I hate the word 'prawns'. The Americans say 'shrimp' and I quite like that. When using a fan-assisted oven, decrease the temperature and cooking time accordingly.

A final rule - rebellious members of the family (young and old) must flick through these pages: gastronomy, you see, is the greatest therapy to which any misfit can be exposed. And I should know.

I hope this little cookbook brings as much enjoyment to the person who is doing the cooking as it surely will to the person who is doing the eating. Me? I'm off to lunch at Wheeler's of St James's...

You're going to see a lot of herbs in this book. Why? Because they are fresh, vibrant, add colour and create flavour. The avocado with fresh herbs was inspired by a trip to Jamaica. Avocados are gigantic in Jamaica, and their shape resembles the island's green hills. There are lots of easy starters here too. The smoked salmon is presented just the way it was when I was a teenager and worked in the kitchen at The Box Tree. But simplicity is the key – nothing in this chapter is too complicated.

Starters

Avocado with fresh crab and herbs

Serves 1

About 50g white crab meat
Lemon juice
Maldon salt
Extra virgin olive oil
1 avocado
Fresh herbs of your choice,
  to garnish

1 Season the crab meat to your taste with a drop or three of lemon juice, a little salt and olive oil.
2 Carefully peel the avocado and slice it in half horizontally, so that you end up with a top and a bottom. Remove the stone and slice away the base so that the avocado bottom is flat underneath and can stand up on a plate.
3 Fill the centre of the avocado with crab meat and put the top half of the avocado on the crab meat.
4 Using a pastry brush, paint olive oil on to the avocado and onto the herbs. Stick the herbs on to the side – the oil should hold them.

Smoked salmon

Serves 1

1 Wallpaper a plate with a single layer of smoked salmon. Use kitchen scissors to remove the overlap by cutting around the rim of the plate. Eat the overlapping salmon – that's the cook's treat.
2 Serve with the lemon in the centre of the plate, ready to be squeezed over the fish.

About 180g good quality
    smoked salmon
½ lemon, wrapped in muslin

Carpaccio of yellowfin tuna à la Niçoise

Serves 2

About 30g tapenade
Extra virgin olive oil
20g red peppers from a
    jar, drained and diced
½ courgette, finely sliced
    and diced
2 slices of very fresh tuna,
    about 80g each
Fresh basil and coriander
    (or fresh herbs of your
    choice), to garnish
1 lemon

1 Mix the tapenade with a tablespoon of olive oil and set aside. Pour a tablespoon of olive oil over the red peppers and set aside.
2 Blanch the courgette by putting it into a saucepan of boiling water for 20 seconds. Quickly refresh the courgette by draining it in a colander and immediately running it under cold water for a few seconds. Set aside.
3 Flatten the tuna slices by putting the fish in the middle of a large chopping board and covering with a layer of clingfilm. Using the base of a saucepan (or, if you have one, a meat hammer), bash the tuna to flatten it. Ideally, the bashing should increase the surface area of the tuna by two or three times, so that it's about the depth of a £1 coin.
4 Carefully use the clingfilm to transfer the fish to a plate, then peel it away. Pour a teaspoon of olive oil onto the tuna and, using your fingers or a pastry brush, rub or brush it into the fish so that the surface glistens.
5 Spread the tapenade across the tuna and scatter over the diced pepper, diced courgette and basil or coriander. Add a dash of the olive oil and give the lemon a squeeze or two over the fish.

By the way… Tapenade is very salty so be sure to taste the dish before seasoning with salt.

14

Carpaccio of yellowfin tuna with ginger and coriander

Serves 1

1 Flatten the tuna by putting the fish in the middle of a large chopping board and covering it with a layer of clingfilm. Using the base of a saucepan (or, if you have one, a meat hammer), bash the tuna to flatten it. Ideally, the bashing should increase the surface area of the tuna by two or three times, so that it's about the depth of a £1 coin.

2 Carefully use the clingfilm to transfer the fish to a plate and peel it away. Pour the soy sauce into the centre of the tuna and rub it over the tuna with your fingers or a pastry brush until the fish is coated. Put the ginger matchsticks onto the fish and drizzle it with olive oil (or toasted sesame if you prefer). Scatter over the coriander leaves.

By the way… You can make the carpaccio of tuna in the morning and then add the oil and herbs before taking to the table.

1 slice of very fresh tuna, about 80g
1 teaspoon light soy sauce
1 piece of fresh ginger, peeled and cut lengthways into matchsticks
Extra virgin olive oil or toasted sesame oil
Handful of fresh coriander leaves (or fresh herbs of your choice), to garnish

17

Gravlax with mustard dressing

Serves 1

300ml water
200ml vinegar
100g sugar
¼ cucumber, peeled,
   deseeded and finely sliced
About 180g gravlax salmon
Baby fennel leaves (or fresh
   herbs of your choice),
   to garnish

For the mustard dressing
4 egg yolks
½ litre vegetable oil
4 heaped tablespoons
   Dijon mustard
4 tablespoons white
   wine vinegar
2 tablespoons caster
   sugar
Maldon sea salt

1 In a saucepan bring to the boil the water, vinegar and sugar, and then remove the pan from the heat. Leave to cool down for a minute or two before pouring the mixture over the sliced cucumber.
2 Make the dressing by whisking together all of the mustard dressing ingredients.
3 Wallpaper the plate with the gravlax and use kitchen scissors to trim around the rim of the plate. Eat the trimmings.
4 Arrange the cucumber slices on top of each other in the middle of the gravlax and scatter the baby fennel leaves on and around the cucumber.
5 Dress the gravlax with the mustard dressing.

Steak tartare Americaine

Serves 4

3 tablespoons tomato ketchup
20 drops Tabasco
4 teaspoons Hellmann's
  mayonnaise
4 tablespoons Worcestershire
  sauce
1 teaspoon mustard
2 teaspoons mashed
  anchovies
4 teaspoons chopped
  cornichons
4 teaspoons finely chopped
  shallots
4 teaspoons capers
450g rump steak, trimmed
  and minced (ask the butcher
  to do this for you)
4 eggs
Black pepper
Maldon sea salt
Fresh flat-leaf parsley
  (or fresh herbs of your
  choice), to garnish

1 Add all the ingredients, except the eggs, seasoning and parsley, to the minced steak and mix thoroughly.
2 Divide into four and make nice neat shapes. Make a little dip with a spoon in the top of each one. Crack the eggs, separate them, and put each yolk in a half shell on top of each portion of beef.
3 Add a twist of black pepper, a pinch of sea salt and a little parsley, to serve.

Salad of boiled ham and mushrooms with parsley

Serves 1

80g good quality ham
A handful of closed cup
   mushrooms
Sherry vinegar, to your taste
Extra virgin olive oil, to
   your taste
Fresh flat-leaf parsley
   (or herbs of your choice),
   to garnish

1 Finely slice the ham into strips the size of matchsticks. Finely slice the mushrooms to the same size.
2 Bring the ham and mushrooms together in a bowl and gently mix together with your fingertips. Drizzle over the sherry vinegar and olive oil and mix with your fingertips. Scatter parsley over the plate before eating.

Salade Lyonnaise

Serves 1

1 In a non-stick frying pan, fry the diced bacon until perfect for you.

2 Don't bother about making a vinaigrette dressing, just splash the frisée leaves with olive oil and then white wine vinegar. Using your hands, toss the salad so that the oil and vinegar coat the leaves. Now poach the egg.

3 In a bowl, assemble the salad like this: frisée, croûtons, perch the poached egg on top of the croûtons, then sprinkle over the bacon and the parsley or chervil. Top with a splash of olive oil, a pinch of sea salt, and finally, flick half a pinch of black pepper onto the white of the egg.

1 rasher good quality streaky bacon, diced
Extra virgin olive oil, for frying and dressing
½ frisée salad (also known as curly endive), heart only
White wine vinegar
1 egg
Croûtons
Fresh parsley or chervil (or fresh herbs of your choice), to garnish
Maldon sea salt and cracked black pepper

Beetroot and goat's cheese salad with walnuts

Serves 2

1 large (or 2 medium-sized) cooked beetroot
1 teaspoon Merlot vinegar
1 teaspoon extra virgin olive oil
40g-60g goat's cheese, broken into large crumbs
1 walnut, chopped into small pieces
Fresh herbs of your choice, to garnish

1 Finely slice the beetroot into circles and arrange the slices on a plate so that they slightly overlap each other.

2 Pour the teaspoon of vinegar onto the beetroot, in the centre of the plate. Using your fingertips or a pastry brush, spread it over the beetroot. Now pour the teaspoon of olive oil into the centre of the plate and again, using your fingertips or a pastry brush, spread it over the beetroot – it will add flavour and make the beet glisten. Scatter over the goat's cheese, chopped walnut and fresh herbs.

By the way…Ideally, a mandolin will slice the beetroot to the perfect width. The beetroot can be sliced, clingfilmed and stored in the fridge ahead of making the salad. If you don't have Merlot to hand, use a vinegar that you like.

Devils on horseback

Serves 10–20

Tabasco sauce, to your taste
200g mango chutney
20 rashers good-quality
  streaky bacon
20 Agen prunes, stoned

1 Preheat the grill. Add 5–10 drops of Tabasco to the mango chutney and taste it, adding more Tabasco if required.

2 Lay out the bacon rashers on a board. Spoon a dollop of the chutney mixture onto each rasher and put a prune on top. Roll up tight and cook them under the grill, turning once or twice, until the bacon has caramelised to your taste.

Pear and endive salad with Gorgonzola and walnuts

Serves 2

1 Finely slice the endive lengthways. Slice the pear lengthways into quarters and then slice each quarter into matchsticks. Cut the walnut into a dozen or so little pieces.

2 Put the pear matchsticks and sliced endive into a mixing bowl and pour over the walnut oil, followed by the sherry vinegar. Sprinkle with a pinch of sea salt. Use your fingers to mix gently, so that the pear and endive are coated in the flavours of the walnut oil and sherry vinegar.

3 Now simply build up the salad on the plates: first, endive, then cubes of Gorgonzola, then scatter over the chopped walnut, a little more endive, followed by more Gorgonzola… and continue to build. Finish by scattering over the parsley.

1 endive
1 pear
1 walnut, chopped into
    small pieces
1 dessertspoon walnut oil
1 teaspoon sherry vinegar
    (or vinegar of your choice)
Maldon sea salt
80g Gorgonzola cheese,
    cut into cubes
Fresh flat-leaf parsley (or
    fresh herbs of your choice),
    to garnish

By the way… The sweetness of the pear contrasts with the bitterness of the cheese. Roquefort can be used instead of Gorgonzola, though I prefer the latter. Similarly, I like Comice pears, but use your favourite variety – though for this salad, make sure the fruit is perfectly ripe. When mixing a salad with your fingers gentlessness is crucial – the ingredients have done you no harm so why rough them up?

31

Gulls' eggs with mayonnaise and celery salt

Serves 4–6

12 gulls' eggs
Celery salt
Hellmann's mayonnaise,
    to serve

1 Put the eggs into a pan of simmering water and cook for 5 minutes and 10 seconds.
2 Remove the pan from the heat and run the eggs under cold water while half peeling them.
3 Spread enough celery salt over a large serving plate to cover, then arrange the eggs on top. Serve with mayonnaise for dipping into.

By the way… If you like, let the mayonnaise down with a little white wine vinegar. If gulls' eggs are unavailable, go for bantam eggs.

Fillet of salmon ketchup and herbs

Serves 2–4

2 salmon fillets
Extra virgin olive oil
 (or clarified butter)
Fresh herbs of your choice,
 to garnish

For the sauce
170g tomato ketchup
50g finely chopped shallots
1 tablespoon chopped
 fresh chives
1 tablespoon chopped
 fresh tarragon
1 tablespoon chopped
 fresh chervil
2 tablespoons Lea & Perrins
 Worcestershire sauce
About 10 drops Tabasco sauce
2 tablespoons white wine
 vinegar
Maldon sea salt
150ml extra virgin olive oil

1 To make the sauce, mix all the ingredients together.
2 Cook the salmon fillets (starting skin-side down) in olive oil or butter in a large frying pan for a few minutes on each side, or longer depending on their thickness.
3 Put the fillets on a plate, skin-side up, and pour over the sauce. Garnish with soft herbs – be it, basil, parsley, or whatever you like.

By the way…Admittedly, the ketchup sauce contains quite a few ingredients but it takes no time to rustle up and and once tasted you will want to make it again. The sauce can be stored in the fridge but will separate after an hour or two. Perhaps make extra for Chicken ketchup, the recipe of which can be found by flicking forward to the Poultry section.

I don't like the word prawns. I much prefer shrimp, as the Americans say. In this chapter you'll find seven dishes devoted to what I call shrimp, and my particular favourite is shrimp with whisky and girolles – it's all about earthiness and the sea, and I think it works extremely well.

The trick is to cook them rapidly, thereby ensuring their flavour and succulence. Likewise, my recipe for moules marinière involves just a few minutes at the hob…and is made, unusually, with no cream.

Shellfish

★ ★ ★

Fresh Cornish crab with herbs

Serves 1

About 100g brown crab meat
Lea & Perrins Worcestershire
 sauce
Tabasco sauce
100g white crab meat
Maldon sea salt
Lemon juice
Extra virgin olive oil
Meat of 2 crab claws, diced
Crispy Sardinian bread,
 or a bread of your choice
Fresh herbs of your choice,
 to garnish

1 Season the brown crab meat with Worcestershire sauce and Tabasco to your taste. Season the white crab meat with salt, a squeeze of lemon and a splash of olive oil.

2 Arrange the white crab meat on the plate and put the empty claws around it. Spoon the brown crab meat onto the other side of the plate. Place the crispy Sardinian bread between the white and brown meat.

3 Dot the plate with the diced crab claw and drizzle the bread with olive oil. Dress the plate with fresh herbs – be it basil, fresh mint or parsley. Season with salt before serving.

Fresh Cornish crab with ginger, pink grapefruit and coriander

Serves 1

About 100g white crab meat
Maldon sea salt
Extra virgin olive oil
½ pink grapefruit
100g brown crab meat
A pinch of curry powder
Meat of 2 crab claws, sliced
1 small piece of fresh ginger,
   peeled and finely sliced
   into wafer-thin matchsticks
Crispy Sardinian bread,
   or bread of your choice
Fresh coriander leaves and
   chives (or fresh herbs of
   your choice), to garnish

1 Season the white crab meat to your taste with a pinch of salt then drizzle over the olive oil and a squeeze of pink grapefruit juice.

2 Arrange the white and brown crab meat on the plate, keeping the meat separate.

3 Peel the grapefruit and cut into segments and then dice each segment.

4 Sprinkle over the curry powder, as if it were a seasoning – again, it's to your taste. Garnish with the grapefruit, ginger, coriander and chives and dot the sliced crab claw around the plate. Put the Sardinian bread between the white and brown meat and flick a pinch of salt over the bread.

Fresh Cornish crab with peas and herbs

Serves 1

About 100g brown crab meat
Lea & Perrins Worcestershire
    sauce
Tabasco sauce
About 100g white crab meat
Extra virgin olive oil
1 lemon
Crispy Sardinian bread,
    or a bread of your choice
A handful of fresh peas
Meat of 2 crab claws, diced
Fresh mint leaves and chives
    (or fresh herbs of your
    choice), to garnish

1 Season the brown crab meat with Worcestershire sauce and Tabasco to your taste. Season the white meat to your taste with olive oil and lemon juice.
2 Assemble on the plate: the brown crab meat, the bread in the middle and the white crab meat on top of the peas. Scatter the claw meat around the dish and garnish with the mint and chives.

Ceviche of scallops with lime, ginger and coriander

Serves 1 (or makes a starter for 2)

1 Finely slice each scallop horizontally into 6 circular slices.

2 Squeeze a few drops of lime juice onto a plate and then, using your fingers, rub the juice over the surface of the plate. Pour about a tablespoon of olive oil onto the plate and again, with your fingers, rub it around.

3 Starting from the rim of the plate, arrange the scallop slices in circles, working your way to the centre.

4 Pour a tablespoon or two of olive oil on top of the scallops and, using those fingers once again, gently massage the oil into the fish. OK, use a pastry brush if you must. Squeeze lime juice over the scallops and massage in.

5 Arrange the ginger matchsticks on top of the scallops – think of the ginger as a seasoning, you don't want it to be overpowering. Scatter over the coriander and a pinch of sea salt before serving.

3 medium-sized scallops
1 piece of fresh ginger, unpeeled and cut lengthways to the size of wafer-thin matchsticks
1 lime
Extra virgin olive oil
Fresh coriander leaves, chopped, to garnish
Maldon sea salt

By the way… This is a dish of delicate flavours. Lime pulp, which is slightly salty, can be used instead of lime juice.

Ceviche of scallops, Oriental-style

Serves 1 (or makes a starter for 2)

3 medium-sized scallops
1 tablespoon light soy sauce
½ tablespoon extra virgin
  olive oil
1 tablespoon toasted
  sesame oil
1 red chilli, finely chopped
1 small piece of fresh ginger,
  sliced lengthways into
  wafer-thin matchsticks
Fresh coriander leaves and
  chives (or fresh herbs of
  your choice), to garnish

1 Finely cut each scallop horizontally into 6 circular slices.
2 Pour half the toasted sesame oil onto a plate and then, using your fingers or a pastry brush, rub or brush it over the surface of the plate.
3 Combine the soy sauce, olive oil and the remaining toasted sesame oil. Add the chilli and then brush the scallops with the flavoursome soy-oil-chilli mixture.
4 Starting from the rim of the plate, arrange the scallops in circles. Arrange the ginger on top of the scallops – remember to think of the ginger as a seasoning, so don't over do it. Scatter the coriander over the top and drop on the sliced chives.

By the way… As with the ceviche of scallops with lime and ginger (see page 45), this works well served on a large platter – use eight large scallops and put the platter in the middle of the table so that guests can help themselves. Soy sauce can overpower dishes so I 'dilute' it with olive oil.

Moules marinière, classic

Serves 2

1kg live mussels
100g unsalted butter, softened
100ml extra virgin olive oil
100ml white wine
3 sprigs of fresh thyme and
   2 bay leaves (or fresh herbs
   of your choice), to garnish

1 Give yourself 5 minutes to clean the mussels like this… running them under cold water, remove any loose grit from the shells and pull away the green beards. You only want to cook the mussels that are alive. To find out if the mussels are dead or alive tap them gently; if the shells close they are alive. If the shells don't move, discard them, and toast your good health.

2 In a small mixing bowl, whisk the butter with the olive oil then set aside.

3 Heat a casserole or a large saucepan with a lid. Pour in the wine and let it boil for about 30 seconds. Now add the mussels and slam on the lid. Steam over a medium-high heat for 2, 3, or even 4 minutes until all the mussels have opened. Discard any mussels that are still closed and toast your good health again.

4 Remove the pan from the heat and stir in the butter mixture so that it coats the fish and the shells. Shake the pan to ensure the mussels are buttery.

5 Add the thyme and bay leaves. Replace the lid and give the pan another good shake to spread the flavours and bouquet of the herbs. Serve immediately.

Shrimps with whisky and girolles

Serves 4

1 Finely slice the girolles, keeping the shape of the mushrooms.

2 In a large frying pan, heat a generous amount of olive oil and fry the shrimps for a minute or so until they are golden and caramelised on one side. Turn the shrimps over to fry the other side and add the mushrooms to the pan. Continue to fry for another minute or so.

3 Throw in the whisky, toss the shrimps and mushrooms and stand back while the alcohol ignites and burns away. Add the stock and the butter. Now stir until the shrimps are golden brown and glazed in butteriness.

4 Scatter over the fresh herbs and salt and pepper, and serve from the pan at the table.

2 handfuls of girolle mushrooms
Extra virgin olive oil
15–20 large shrimps
A splash of whisky
A splash of Knorr concentrated chicken stock
A knob of unsalted butter
Fresh herbs of your choice, to garnish
Maldon sea salt and black pepper

By the way... I love girolles and they work well with the whisky, but use your favourite wild mushrooms for this dish. The whisky needs to be peaty for the dish to be perfect – try something like Laphroaig. Taste this dish before seasoning, as Knorr stock is salty.

Six more ways with shrimp

Serves 4

16-20 shrimps
Extra virgin olive oil

To cook the shrimps, fry in the olive oil for a
minute or so on each side until nicely coloured.

Shrimps with Pernod and garlic butter

Top left

A splash of Pernod
50g unsalted butter
Cloves of crushed garlic, to your taste
½ handful of fresh parsley, finely chopped

1 Make the garlic butter by mashing
together the ingredients and set aside.
2 Fry the shrimps as before. At the end
add a splash of Pernod. Toss the shrimps
and add the garlic butter.
3 Scatter over the herbs before serving.

Shrimps with paprika and garlic

Bottom left

Finely sliced garlic, as much as you like
2 teaspoons of paprika

Fry the shrimps as before but add
the garlic. Stir in the paprika at the
end of cooking.

Shrimps with curry powder and rosemary

Top right

Mild curry powder, to your taste
1 sprig of fresh rosemary, leaves only, chopped

Sprinkle curry powder over the shrimps
as if you were seasoning and fry as before.
Stir in the chopped rosemary leaves
towards the end of cooking. Stir and serve.

Oriental-style

Bottom right

2 spring onions, coarsely chopped
1 piece of fresh ginger, peeled and
    coarsely chopped

1 Fry the shrimps as before.
2 Remove from the heat and stir
in the spring onions and ginger.

Salt and pepper shrimps

Top

Finely cracked black pepper
Maldon sea salt
Fresh parsley, finely chopped
50g unsalted butter
Fresh thyme leaves, chopped
Fresh rosemary leaves, chopped

1 Make the herb butter by mixing the
parsley with the butter and adding a little
of the thyme and rosemary.
2 Coat one side of the shrimps in the
black pepper and then fry as before.
3 Remove from the heat, stir in the herb
butter and season with sea salt. Serve
the pan at the table.

Shrimps with fresh herbs

Bottom

Fresh parsley, finely chopped
50g butter
Fresh thyme leaves, chopped
Fresh rosemary leaves, chopped
Finely shallots, sliced

1 Make the herb butter by mixing
together all the ingredients and set aside.
2 In a large saucepan and on a medium-high
heat, fry the shrimps as before.
3 Remove the pan from the heat, immediately
stir in the herb butter and serve from the pan.

*By the way…My recipe for herb butter is
merely a guide – adjust to your taste. For my
recipe I use 80 per cent parsley, 10 per cent
finely sliced shallots, 5 per cent thyme and
5 per cent rosemary.*

We all know fish and lemon works. But what about fish and orange? Halibut and orange: two ingredients. Bring them together and you're looking at the perfect summer lunch, but have you ever heard of a simpler dish to make?

You can't mess up these fish dishes and the sea bass en papillote – once tried and it will become a favourite in your home.

Fish

Wild halibut steak à la Niçoise

Serves 2

8 black olives, stoned
2 anchovy fillets
1 tomato, diced
Extra virgin olive oil
2 halibut steaks, about
    200g each
A handful of fresh basil
    or coriander leaves (or
    herbs of your choice),
    to garnish
1 lemon

1 Slice each olive lengthways into 3 segments and then slice each segment again lengthways into two or 3 pieces so that they look like petals. Set aside. Slice each anchovy fillet lengthways into 5 strips. Set aside.
2 Fry the diced tomato in olive oil for a minute or so, but not to the point of collapse.
3 In a large pan, fry the halibut steaks in olive oil for 3–4 minutes on each side, or longer depending on the thickness of the steaks, until golden.
4 Remove from the pan and assemble on the plates like this: place the halibut on the plate, criss-cross the anchovies on top of the halibut then spoon over the tomatoes and olives.
5 Scatter with herbs and be generous – this dish is, after all, from the south of France. Finish with a squeeze of lemon juice on the fish and a drizzle of extra virgin olive oil.

Wild halibut steak Grenobloise

Serves 2

3 tablespoons extra virgin
    olive oil, for dressing
    and frying
2 teaspoons capers
1 lemon, peeled and diced
½ small Cucumber
80g shrimps
2 halibut steaks, about
    200g each
A handful of fresh parsley
    (or fresh herbs of your
    choice), to garnish

1 Pour one tablespoon of olive oil over the capers and leave in a warm place in the kitchen.
2 Pour another tablespoon of olive oil over the diced lemon and set aside in a warm place in the kitchen. Dice the cucumber and blanch in a saucepan of boiling water for 30 seconds. Drain and leave in a warm place in the kitchen.
3 Warm the shrimps in a pan of olive oil for 2–3 minutes.
4 In a large frying pan, cook the halibut steaks in the remaining olive oil for about 3 minutes on each side, or longer depending on the thickness of the steaks, until golden brown.
5 Serve the steaks and shrimps garnished with the capers, lemon, cucumber and parsley.

Wild halibut steak Provençale

Serves 2

1 Slice each olive lengthways into 3 segments and then slice each segment again lengthways into 2 or 3 pieces, so that they look like petals. Set aside.

2 Blanch the tomatoes in a bowl of boiling water for 30 seconds and then drain and leave them for 5 minutes to cool. Remove the skins, deseed and dice the flesh, and set aside.

3 Make a dressing by combining a couple of tablespoons of olive oil with the lemon juice.

4 Heat the remaining olive oil in a large frying pan and cook the halibut for about 3 minutes on each side, or depending on the thickness of the steaks, until golden brown and delicious.

5 Pour the dressing into the frying pan and bring to the boil. Add the tomatoes and basil, just to soften them a little, and remove the pan from the heat.

6 Garnish the fish with the olive petals, diced tomatoes and basil leaves. Serve the remaining dressing separately in a sauce-boat. Quick, invigorating and glorious.

8 black olives, stoned
2 plum tomatoes
4 tablespoons extra virgin olive oil, for frying and dressing
1 tablespoon lemon juice
2 halibut steaks, about 200g each
6 large fresh basil leaves, each torn in half, to garnish

Four more ways with halibut steak

Serves 2

Extra virgin olive oil
Unsalted butter
2 halibut steaks, about 200g each
Fresh herbs of your choice, to garnish
Maldon sea salt

For all of the dishes below, fry the halibut in olive oil or butter for about 4 minutes on each side, or longer depending on the thickness. Use your senses: a nice sizzle and an appetising colour are good signs.

with oranges
Top left

7 oranges

1 Peel and cut one orange into segments, and place in a bow with a splash of olive oil. Juice the remaining 6.
2 Cook the halibut as described before.
3 The final bit… Pour the orange juice into the same pan and reduce to about 4 teaspoons of orange essence, shaking well every 20 seconds or so.
4 Assemble on the plate like this: fish, the reduced juice and a few orange dice on top, then chopped herbs and a sprinkling of salt.

with porcini
Bottom left

2 handfuls of porcini mushrooms
  (or wild mushrooms of your choice)
Balsamic vinegar

1 Slice the porcini into quarters.
2 Cook the halibut as described before.
3 Using the same pan, fry the porcini slices for a minute in olive oil.
4 To finish, the fish and porcini should be drizzled with 1 teaspoon of balsamic vinegar mixed with the oil from the pan. Scatter fresh herbs (coriander works well here) and season with salt.

tartare
Top right

4 tablespoons Hellmann's mayonnaise
1 tablespoon chopped gherkins
1 tablespoon capers, finely chopped
1 tablespoon chopped shallots

1 Make the tartare sauce by combining the sauce ingredients. Allow it to chill.
2 Cook the halibut as described before.
3 Spoon or pipe the tartare sauce over the fish and scatter with herbs.

with cucumber and ginger
Bottom right

1 lime, peeled, cut into segments and diced
  into triangles
4 slices of fresh ginger, sliced into matchsticks
½ cucumber, peeled and diced

1 Mix the lime with a tablespoon of olive oil and set aside.
2 Cook the halibut as described before.
3 Blanch the ginger matchsticks in boiling water for about a minute. Remove from the pan, keeping the boiling water, and quickly refresh in cold water for a few seconds.
4 Add the diced cucumber to the saucepan and boil for 30 seconds. Quickly refresh and set aside. Spoon the cucumber over the fish and arrange the ginger and herbs on top (coriander works well here).

Yellowfin tuna steak à la Niçoise

Serves 2

8 black olives, stoned
8 green olives, stoned
2 teaspoons capers
8 cherry tomatoes, halved
2 tuna steaks, about 180g each
Extra virgin olive oil
Maldon sea salt
Fresh herbs of your choice,
  to garnish

1 Slice each olive lengthways into 3 segments and then slice each segment lengthways again into 2 or 3 pieces so that they look like petals. Set aside.
2 Make the garnish by combining the capers, the olive petals and the tomatoes. Leave in a warm part of the kitchen (or even outside in the sun, if it's a nice day) for an hour or so.
3 Rub each side of the tuna steaks with olive oil or brush with a pastry brush.
4 Add half a pinch of salt evenly to the fish, then fry in a dry pan for about 90 seconds on each side, or longer depending on the thickness of the steaks.
5 Garnish with the olives, capers, tomatoes and fresh herbs and serve.

Yellowfin tuna steak
à la Sicilienne

Serves 2

1 lemon
4 tablespoons extra virgin
  olive oil, for dressing
  and frying
10 black olives, stoned
2 teaspoons capers
2 tuna steaks, about 180g each
4 fresh basil leaves, halved
Fresh herbs of your choice,
  to garnish
Maldon sea salt

1 Squeeze the juice of half the lemon and set aside.
2 Cut the remaining lemon half into wedges and then dice the flesh.
3 Pour about 1 tablespoon of olive oil over the diced lemon and keep this mixture in a warm part of the kitchen.
4 Slice each olive lengthways into three segments and then slice each segment lengthways again into two or three pieces, so that they look like petals.
5 Pour a tablespoon of olive oil over the petals, just to soften them. Set aside in a warm place.
6 Pour a tablespoon of olive oil over the capers and set aside.
7 When you are ready to eat, heat a large frying pan. Rub each side of the tuna steaks with olive oil or brush with a pastry brush. Season the fish with half a pinch of salt just before it goes into the dry pan. Fry for about 90 seconds on each side, or longer depending on the thickness of the steaks.
8 Remove the fish from the frying pan and arrange on a plate: first the tuna, then the lemon pieces and sprinkle on the capers, the olive petals and basil and herbs. Finish with a pinch of Maldon sea salt.

Yellowfin tuna steak with wild rocket and vintage balsamico

Serves 2

2 tuna steaks, about 180g each
A handful of fresh flat-leaf
  parsley (or fresh herbs of
  your choice), to garnish
Maldon sea salt
2 handfuls of wild rocket
Extra virgin olive oil
Vintage balsamic vinegar

1 Rub each side of the tuna steaks with olive oil or brush with a pastry brush.

2 Finely chop the parsley and pat it on to the tuna. Season the fish with half a pinch of salt just before it goes into the dry pan. Fry for about 90 seconds on each side, or longer depending on the thickness of the steaks.

3 Remove the fish and place on serving plates. Combine a teaspoon of olive oil with the pan juices and stir.

4 Garnish the fish with the wild rocket, pour over a splash of the olive oil from the pan and a splash of balsamic vinegar, and serve.

By the way…I love vintage balsamico and would highly recommend it. If non-vintage balsamic vinegar is the only vinegar in your larder then don't worry – it's still delicious.

Yellowfin tuna steak, Oriental-style

Serves 2

1 teaspoon dark soy sauce
Extra virgin olive oil, for
    dressing and brushing
1 teaspoon toasted sesame oil
1 piece fresh ginger, peeled
    and cut lengthways into
    matchsticks
Spring onions, sliced
    lengthways
2 tuna steaks, about 180g each
Maldon sea salt
Fresh herbs of your choice,
    to garnish

1 Make a dressing by combining the soy sauce, a teaspoon of olive oil and sesame oil.

2 Blanch the ginger matchsticks by putting them into a saucepan of boiling water for 20 seconds. As soon as the water boils, drain the ginger, pouring the hot water momentarily over the spring onions, just enough to soften them. Refresh the ginger by holding it under cold water for a few seconds. Pour the dressing over the ginger and spring onions and set aside.

3 Rub each side of the tuna steaks with olive oil or brush with a pastry brush. Season the fish with half a pinch of salt just before it goes into the dry pan. Fry for about 90 seconds on each side, or longer depending on the thickness of the steaks.

4 Serve with the ginger and spring onions on top and around the tuna steaks.

A whole sea bass roasted for about 12 minutes and garnished with wild mushrooms

Serves 2

4 tablespoons extra virgin
   olive oil
1 whole sea bass, about 1kg
150g wild mushrooms
Clarified butter
Fresh parsley, finely chopped

1 Preheat the oven to 190°C/gas 5.
2 Heat the olive oil in a roasting tin on the hob and then lay the sea bass in the tin. Fry for a couple of minutes until one side of the fish is slightly browned. Carefully lift the fish by its gills, turn it over and caramelise the other side.
3 Transfer the fish to the oven and roast for 12–15 minutes.
4 While the bass is in the oven, finely slice the mushrooms and fry them for a couple of minutes in butter.
5 Serve from the roasting tin, garnishing the fish with the mushrooms and parsley. Mix the buttery juices from the mushroom pan with the juices from the roasting tin and pour this flavoursome mixture over the fish. Unbeatable.

Sea bass flavoured with curry, roasted for about 12 minutes and finished with Sauternes and fresh coriander

Serves 2

1 Preheat the oven to 190°C/gas 5.

2 Season both sides of the bass generously with a good dusting of the curry powder. Heat 5–6 tablespoons of olive oil in a roasting tin on the hob and then lay the sea bass in the tin so that the fish begins to turn golden. Holding the fish by its gills, turn it and begin to brown the other side.

3 Arrange the bay leaves, thyme, star anise and coriander seeds on top of the bass, and sprinkle a pinch of curry powder into the oil around the fish. Continue to cook on the hob for a minute so that both sides have browned a bit. Transfer the fish to the oven to roast for 12 minutes.

4 Meanwhile, in a saucepan, boil the Sauternes until it has evaporated and reduced in volume by about two-thirds; this should take a few minutes.

5 Serve the fish from the roasting tin – garnish with the coriander and pour the syrupy, reduced Sauternes onto the fish at the table.

1 whole sea bass, about 1 kg
A generous amount of mild curry powder
Extra virgin olive oil
3 bay leaves
4 sprigs of fresh thyme
3 whole star anise
1 teaspoon coriander seeds, crushed
100ml Sauternes (or another dessert wine)
Fresh coriander (or fresh herbs of your choice), to garnish

A whole sea bass with lots of aniseed flavours, cooked en papillote for about 15 minutes

Serves 2

Extra virgin olive oil
1 whole sea bass, about 1kg
¼ small fennel bulb, peeled
  and cut into julienne slices
2 whole star anise
A splash of Pernod (or Ricard)
1 lemon, for squeezing
Maldon sea salt
Fresh tarragon and coriander
  (or fresh herbs of your
  choice), to garnish

1 Preheat the oven to 190°C/gas 5.
2 Lay a piece of foil that is at least twice the size the fish on the work surface. Pour about a teaspoon of olive oil into the centre of the foil and rub it around – just enough to stop the fish sticking to the foil.
3 Lay the sea bass onto the centre of the foil and arrange the fennel and star anise on top of the fish. Add the splash of Pernod.
4 Fold the foil and scrunch the edges of the foil to seal, so that the flavours will be captured within. It should be half-moon shaped.
5 Put the foiled fish in a roasting tin and then place it on the hob and cook over a medium heat for a couple of minutes. Transfer the tin straight to the oven and bake for 15 minutes. The foil will puff up and look like a large silver Cornish pasty, or rather, it *should*.
6 Remove the foiled fish from the oven and carefully open the foil at the table. Add a splash of olive oil, a squeeze of lemon, a sprinkling of sea salt, tarragon and coriander.

A whole sea bass with spring onions, ginger, fresh coriander, cooked en papillote for about 15 minutes

Serves 2

1 sea bass, about 1kg
Extra virgin olive oil
1 dessertspoon white wine
1 piece of fresh ginger,
  peeled and finely sliced
  into matchsticks
2 spring onions, finely
  sliced lengthways
Fresh coriander leaves
  (or fresh herbs of your
  choice), to garnish

1 Preheat the oven to 190°C/gas 5.
2 Lay a piece of foil that is large enough to fold over the fish on the work surface. Pour a teaspoon of olive oil into the centre of the foil and rub it around, just enough to stop the fish sticking to the foil during cooking.
3 Lay the sea bass into the centre of the foil and pour over the wine. Fold the foil, and scrunch around the edges so that all the flavours will be captured within. It should now be shaped like a half-moon.
4 Carefully place the foiled fish in a roasting tin and cook over a medium heat on the hob for a couple of minutes. Transfer the tin straight to the oven and bake for 15–17 minutes.
5 Meanwhile, blanch the ginger. As soon as the water boils, drain the ginger, pouring the hot water momentarily over the spring onions, just enough to soften them. Refresh the ginger by holding it under cold water for a few seconds.
6 Remove the foiled fish from the oven and carefully open the foil at the table. Garnish with the ginger, spring onions and coriander before serving.

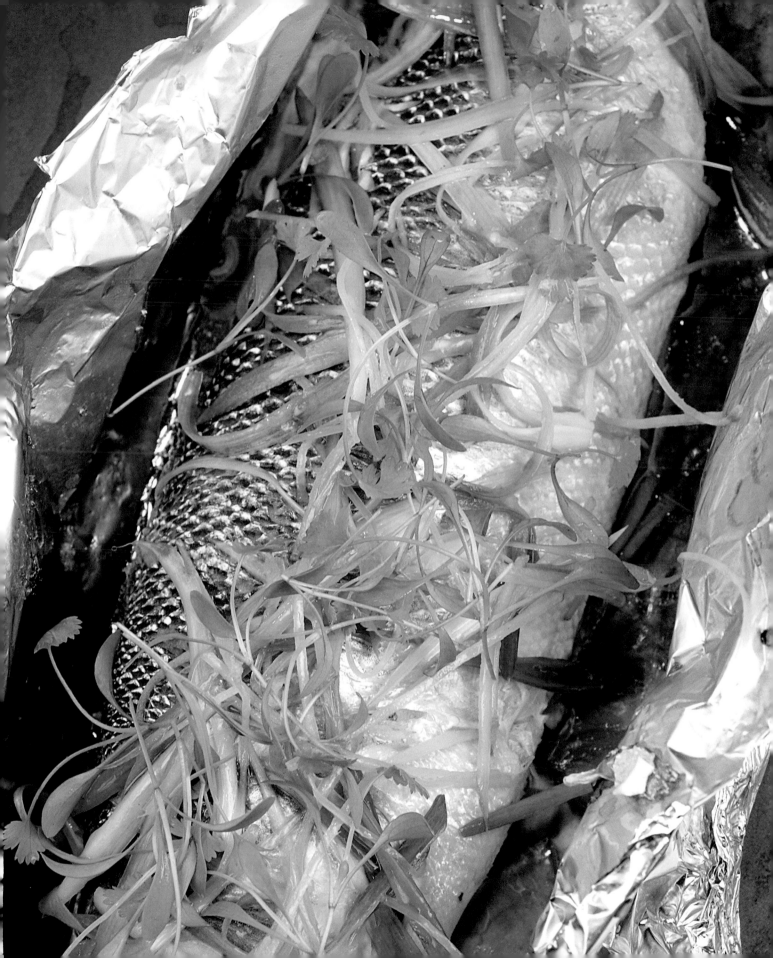

A whole sea bass cooked en papillote and served with clams and chopped parsley

Serves 2

1 whole sea bass, about 1kg
Extra virgin olive oil
50ml white wine
2 bay leaves
2 sprigs of fresh thyme
1 small shallot, diced
A couple of handfuls of clams
A handful of chopped parsley,
  to garnish
Maldon sea salt, just in case

For the butter mixture
150g unsalted butter, softened
150ml extra virgin olive oil

1 Preheat the oven to 190°C/gas 5.
2 For the butter mixture, combine the butter and oil using a hand-whisk and set aside.
3 Lay a piece of foil that is at least twice the size the fish on the work surface. Pour about a teaspoon of olive oil in the centre of the foil and rub it around – just enough to stop the fish sticking to the foil. Lay the sea bass in the centre of the foil. Fold the foil and scrunch it to seal in the flavours. It should be half-moon shaped.
4 Put the foiled fish in a roasting tin and cook it on the hob over a medium heat for a couple of minutes. Transfer the tin straight to the oven and bake for 15–17 minutes. The foil will puff up and look like a large, silver Cornish pasty. That's the idea anyway.
5 Allow yourself a few minutes to steam the clams. In a large saucepan, heat the wine, bay leaves, thyme and shallot and boil rapidly over a high heat for about a minute. Add the clams and put the lid on the pan. They'll be done in a minute or two, at which point add the butter mixture. Shake the pan (with the lid on) or give the clams a stir just to make sure they are buttery. Discard any clams that haven't opened.
6 Serve the sea bass at the table, carefully opening the foil and spoon over the clams, bay leaves and thyme, and the divine sauce. Garnish with chopped parsley. Don't season with salt until you've tasted the fish.

Whole seabream, Oriental-style

Serves 2

1 piece fresh ginger, cut lengthways into matchsticks
Lemon juice
2 spring onions, cut lengthways
1 whole sea bream, about 600g
Extra virgin olive oil
Fresh coriander (or fresh herbs of your choice), to garnish

For the dressing
2 dessertspoons toasted sesame oil
2 dessertspoons light soy sauce
1 red chilli, deseeded and finely sliced

1 Preheat the oven to 190°C/gas 5.

2 Put the ginger and lemon juice into a small saucepan and cover with a splash of water. Bring to the boil, wait 20 seconds and then remove from the heat. As soon as the water boils, drain the ginger, pouring the hot water momentarily over the spring onions, just enough to soften them. Refresh the ginger by holding it under cold water for a few seconds.

3 In a roasting tin on the hob, heat the olive oil and then brown the fish on one side. Turn it, brown the other side and transfer the tin to the oven to roast for 10–12 minutes. While the fish roasts, combine the sesame oil, soy sauce, and chilli.

4 Serve the fish with the ginger and spring onions scattered over, then pour over the soy-oil mixture and sprinkle with coriander.

Red mullet with a sauce of tomato juice and cumin

Serves 2

1 In a large frying pan, shallow-fry the red mullet in some olive oil for about 3 minutes on each side, or longer depending on the size of the fish, until golden.
2 Meanwhile, make the sauce in another pan by bringing to the boil the tomato juice, 1 teaspoon of olive oil and the cumin. Add the butter and stir once. If using celery leaves, shallow fry them in olive oil.
3 Spoon the tomato sauce onto a plate, lay the fish on top of the sauce. Garnish with the celery leaves and serve. Healthy and packed with flavour.

2 whole red mullet, about 100g each
Extra virgin olive oil
100ml tomato juice
A pinch of ground cumin
A knob of unsalted butter
A handful of celery leaves, to garnish

Four more ways with red mullet

Serves 2

2 red mullet, about 100g each
Extra virgin olive oil
A handful of fresh herbs, to garnish

Cook the pair of mullet like this: in a pan, shallow fry them in olive oil over a medium heat for 3-4 minutes on each side (depending on the size of the fish).

with pesto and a few capers

Top left

1 tablespoon pesto
1 teaspoon capers
Maldon sea salt

1 Mix the pesto with two tablespoons of olive oil and add the capers. Set aside until you are ready to cook the fish.
2 Fry the mullet as described above.
3 Remove the fish from the pan and season it with a few crystals of sea salt. Spoon over the pesto-caper sauce; scatter the herbs (torn basil leaves work well here) and serve.

with porcini and a Madeira reduction

Bottom left

50ml Madeira
1 tablespoon truffle oil
1-2 teaspoons Porcini powder
A handful or two of dried porcini

1 In a small saucepan, boil the Madeira until it has evaporated, thickened and reduced in volume to about a dessertspoon. Pour this syrup into a bowl and combine it with the truffle oil.
2 Season the red mullet with a coating of porcini powder. Cook the mullet as described above.
3 Assemble on the plate: first the red mullet, then sprinkle salt. Scatter fresh parsley.

Oriental-style

Top right

2 whole star anise,
1 piece of fresh ginger, unpeeled and sliced to the size of matchsticks
1 large spring onion, finely sliced lengthways

1 Blanch the ginger matchsticks by putting them in a saucepan of water and bringing to the boil. When the water boils count to 10, remove the pan from the heat and drain through a colander, pouring the hot water momentarily over the spring onions, just enough to soften them.
2 Fry the mullet as described at the top of this page.
3 Serve with the star anise, ginger spring onions spooned on and around the fish, and add the herbs.

with tapenade and fresh basil

Bottom right

1 heaped tablespoon tapenade
A handful of basil leaves

1 Thin the tapenade by mixing it with 3 tablespoons of olive oil.
2 Fry the red mullet as described at the top of this page.
3 Serve the fish with the thinned tapenade spooned onto it, and the basil leaves dropped on and around the mullet. then sprinkle salt. Scatter with fresh herbs (finely chopped parsley works well).

I'm giving you lots of steak dishes here because we all love steak. Prefer rump or rib-eye? Then use rump or rib-eye. The roasted calf's liver is very special and again, the double pork chop dishes require only a few ingredients because that pork has to be the star of the show. The more you add the more you take away…

Meat

Peppered steak

Serves 4

4 fillet steaks, about
180g each
Cracked black pepper
3 tablespoons extra
virgin olive oil
100ml Lea & Perrins
Worcestershire sauce
150ml double cream

1 Dust one side of each steak with the pepper so that the pepper sticks to the surface of the meat.
2 In a heavy-based frying pan, heat the olive oil and fry the steaks, pepper-side up, for 3–4 minutes. Turn the steaks and continue to fry for a further 3–4 minutes.
3 Remove the pan from the heat and allow the steaks to rest in the pan in a warm part of the kitchen for 5–10 minutes. Remove the steaks from the pan and put to one side. The juices that are left in the frying pan are delicious, so don't discard them.
4 Meanwhile, make the sauce. First, pour the Worcestershire sauce into the same pan and heat, but don't bring to the boil. Cook until the sauce has reduced by about two-thirds. Now add the cream, keep it on the heat and stir. That's your sauce done.
5 Return the steaks to the hot sauce in the pan and serve.

Fillet steak with shallots and Dijon mustard

Serves 4

50g unsalted butter
4 large shallots, very
    finely sliced (or 2
    medium-sized onions)
Extra virgin olive oil
4 fillet steaks, about
    180g each
Dijon mustard, to your taste
A handful of fresh flat leaf
    parsley, to garnish

1 In a frying pan or sauté pan, melt the butter; add the shallots and sauté them until soft and golden. Drain them in a colander, but keep the butter because you'll need it in a minute.
2 Return the pan to the heat and pour in a tablespoon of olive oil. Add the steaks and fry for 3–4 minutes on each side, turning them only once. Remove the pan from the heat and allow the steaks to rest in the pan in a warm part of the kitchen for 5–10 minutes.
3 Using a pastry brush, paint the Dijon mustard on top of each steak and then spoon on the golden shallots. Reheat the shallot butter and pour it over the steaks. Top with the chopped parsley. Beautiful.

Fillet steak Provençale

Serves 4

4 anchovy fillets
8 green olives per person
1 tablespoon extra virgin
   olive oil
4 fillet steaks, about
   180g each
About 200g tapenade
Fresh herbs of your choice,
   to garnish

1 Slice each anchovy fillet into 5 long strips. Slice the green olives lengthways into 3 segments and then cut each segment into halves (or thirds, depending on size) so that they look like little petals. Set the anchovy strips and olive petals aside while you cook the steaks.
2 In a heavy-based pan, heat the olive oil and fry the steaks for 3–4 minutes on each side until deliciously caramalised, turning them only once. Remove the pan from the heat and allow the steaks to rest in the pan in a warm part of the kitchen for 5–10 minutes.
3 Assemble by spreading the tapenade on each steak, then criss-cross the anchovies over the meat, and to complete the dish, put the olive petals within the criss-crosses, and drop on some fresh herbs.

Fillet steak with snails and garlic butter

Serves 4

1 tablespoon extra virgin
   olive oil
4 fillet steaks, about
   180g each
24 tinned snails
Fresh herbs of your choice,
   to garnish

For the garlic butter
50g unsalted butter, softened
1 garlic clove, crushed and
   puréed
1 tablespoon fresh flat-leaf
   parsley, chopped

1 Make the garlic butter by combining the softened butter with the garlic and parsley.

2 In a heavy-based frying pan, heat the olive oil and fry the steaks for 3–4 minutes on each side, turning them only once. Remove the pan from the heat and allow the steaks to rest in the pan in a warm part of the kitchen for 5–10 minutes.

3 Meanwhile, melt the garlic butter in a pan and add the snails. On a low heat, fry them for a couple of minutes, just to heat them through, but be careful not to burn the butter.

4 Serve each steak with 4 snails. Serve the remaining snails in their own dish, with the juices from the steak pan poured over them.

Fillet steak à la Boston with oysters

Serves 2

Maldon sea salt
½ dessertspoon cracked
  black pepper
2 fillet steaks, about
  180g each
1 tablespoon extra virgin
  olive oil
2 fresh oysters, in their juices
1 lemon, for squeezing
Fresh herbs of your choice,
  to garnish

1 Mix the salt and pepper together on a plate and dust the steaks in the mixture.

2 In a heavy-based frying pan, heat the olive oil and fry the steaks for 3–4 minutes on each side, turning them only once. Remove from the heat and allow the steaks to rest in the pan in a warm part of the kitchen for 5–10 minutes.

3 Meanwhile, pour the oysters and their juices into a hot saucepan and poach them for 30 seconds, just so they are lightly cooked.

4 Serve with an oyster on top of each steak, with a drop or two of olive oil and a squeeze of lemon juice on each oyster. Garnish with the fresh herbs.

Fillet steak with black pepper, raisins secs and a spoon of Armagnac

Serves 2

2 dessertspoons raisins
2 fillet steaks, about
    180g each
½ dessertspoon cracked
    black pepper
1 tablespoon extra virgin
    olive oil
A knob of unsalted butter
1 dessertspoon Armagnac
Fresh herbs of your choice,
    to garnish

1 Put the raisins in a small saucepan, cover with cold water and bring to the boil. Reduce the heat and let the water simmer for about 5 minutes. Remove the pan from the heat, drain the raisins and rinse them under cold water. Set aside.

2 Put the cracked black pepper on a plate and dust the steaks.

3 Heat the olive oil in a heavy-based frying pan and fry the steaks for 3–4 minutes on each side, turning them only once. Remove the pan from the heat and allow the steaks to rest in the pan in a warm part of the kitchen for 5–10 minutes.

4 While the steaks are resting, put the raisins into a hot pan with a knob of butter and cook for a minute or two, before adding the Armagnac and cooking for another 20 or 30 seconds. Serve with the raisins on top of the steak and around it and scatter the fresh herbs.

Steaks with salsa verde and mustard fruits

Serves 2

1 tablespoon extra virgin
  olive oil
2 fillet steaks, about
  180g each
1 tablespoon salsa verde
2 tablespoons mustard fruits
Fresh herbs of your choice,
  to garnish

1 In a heavy-based frying pan or sauté pan, heat the olive oil and fry the steaks for 3–4 minutes on each side, turning them only once. For this dish, the steak is best cooked rare. Remove the pan from the heat and allow the steaks to rest in the pan in a warm part of the kitchen for 5–10 minutes.

2 Assemble on the plate, spooning the salsa verde on top of the steak and the colourful mustard fruits around the beef.

By the way… You can buy ready-made salsa verde but if you prefer to make it yourself, combine the following:

1 tablespoon shallots, finely chopped
1 tablespoon fresh chives, finely chopped
1 tablespoon fresh tarragon, finely chopped
1 tablespoon fresh flat-leaf parsley, finely chopped
1 tablespoon extra fine capers
1 anchovy fillet, finely chopped
½ dessertspoon Merlot vinegar
2 tablespoons extra virgin olive oil

Taste and then add more olive oil and vinegar to your taste, so that it's just perfect for you and your palate.

Fillet steak with wild rocket and vintage balsamico

Serves 2

1 tablespoon extra virgin
   olive oil
2 fillet steaks, about
   180g each
A couple of handfuls of rocket
Pecorino cheese, thinly sliced
Vintage balsamic vinegar

1 In a heavy-based frying pan or sauté pan, heat the olive oil and fry the steaks for about 3 minutes on each side, turning them only once. For this dish, the steak is best cooked rare. Remove the pan from the heat and allow the steaks to rest in the pan in a warm part of the kitchen for 5–10 minutes.

2 Slice the steaks and serve them on a platter with a scattering of rocket on top and around the beef; then add the pecorino. Finish with a splash of olive oil and a drizzle of the vintage balsamico.

Fillet steak with peppercorn sauce

Serves 2

1 In a saucepan, bring the Worcestershire sauce
to the boil and cook for a few minutes until it
reduces in volume by about two-thirds. Remove
the pan from the heat and pour in the cream. Add
the green peppercorns and the pinch of stock cube.
Taste it – nice?

2 In a heavy-based frying pan or sauté pan, heat
the olive oil and fry the steaks for 3–4 minutes on each
side, turning them only once. Remove the pan from the
heat and allow the steaks to rest in a warm part of the
kitchen for 5–10 minutes.

3 Put the steaks in the pan of very nice peppercorn
sauce and serve.

100ml Lea & Perrins
   Worcestershire sauce
100ml double cream
1 teaspoon green
   peppercorns
A pinch of 1 Knorr chicken
   stock cube
1 tablespoon extra virgin
   olive oil
2 fillet steaks, about
   180g each

Fillet steak with porcini and vintage balsamico

Serves 4

250g wild mushrooms
(I have used porcini)
1 tablespoon balsamic
vinegar
Extra virgin olive oil
4 fillet steaks, about
180g each
Fresh herbs of your
choice, to garnish

1 Clean and slice the mushrooms. Make a dressing by mixing the vinegar with 2 tablespoons of olive oil. Set aside.

2 In a heavy-based frying pan, heat a tablespoon of olive oil and fry the steaks for 3–4 minutes on each side, turning them only once. Remove the pan from the heat and allow the steaks to rest in the pan in a warm part of the kitchen for 5–10 minutes.

3 Meanwhile, in another pan, fry the mushrooms in a generous amount of olive oil for a minute or two.

4 Using a pastry brush, paint the meat with the vinegar-oil dressing and scatter the wild mushrooms on and around the steaks. Mix the juices from the mushroom pan with the juices from the pan used to cook the meat, and spoon this lovely sauce over the steaks. Scatter with herbs.

By the way… I've used porcini, but if you can't get hold of them use the wild mushrooms that you like. If you wish, throw in very finely chopped garlic and shallots at the end of cooking.

Fillet steak with morels à la crème

Serves 2

Extra virgin olive oil
2 fillet steaks, about
   180g each
A handful of morels
About 50ml double cream
Fresh herbs of your choice,
   to garnish

1 In a heavy-based frying pan or sauté pan, heat a tablespoon of olive oil and fry the steaks for 3–4 minutes on each side, turning them only once. Remove the pan from the heat and allow the steaks to rest in the pan in a warm part of the kitchen for 5–10 minutes.
2 Meanwhile, in another pan, cook the morels in some olive oil for a minute.
3 Push the morels to one side of the pan and pour the cream into the other side of the pan. Boil the cream over a high heat for a minute or two until it has evaporated and reduced in volume to a tablespoon or so. Now toss the morels in the pan so that they are coated in the creamy reduction.
4 Serve the morels on and around the steaks and scatter with herbs.

Beef brisket in Guinness and prune juice

Serves 4

2 onions, halved
2 garlic cloves, peeled
Extra virgin olive oil
500ml prune juice
550ml Guinness
200ml water
Knorr beef stock cube
1.3kg beef brisket,
    trimmed and cut into
    8 pieces

1 Preheat the oven to 140°C/gas 1.
2 Pulp the onions and garlic in a food processor
(or use a hand-held stick blender) until it is almost
a purée.
3 Heat 1–2 tablespoon of olive oil in a casserole, add
the onion-garlic pulp and fry over a low heat, stirring
frequently, until the purée melts and smells delicious.
It will take 5–6 minutes to cook, but don't brown it.
4 Remove the casserole from the heat and pour in
the prune juice, Guinness, water and stock cube.
Set aside.
5 In a large heavy-based frying pan, heat some olive
oil – be generous with it – and then brown the beef
for a minute or two on each side, turning only once.
Remove the beef pieces from the pan, patting them
dry with kitchen paper.
6 Add the beef to the casserole and cook in the oven
for 4 hours, or until the meat is delicately tender.

*By the way… As an extra garnish, separately
fry prunes and bacon lardons and spoon
them over the beef.*

Roast rump of lamb Dijonnaise with roasting juices

Serves 2

Extra virgin olive oil (or
    clarified butter)
Rump of lamb, about 350g
Dijon mustard, to your taste
A handful of fresh chives,
    diced
Fresh herbs of your choice,
    to garnish

1 Preheat the oven to 180°C/gas 4.

2 Heat the olive oil or butter in a non-stick frying pan and caramelise the lamb on both sides. Transfer the lamb to a roasting tin, skin-side down. Pop it in the oven and roast for 10–15 minutes.

3 Remove the lamb from the oven and allow the meat to rest for 5–10 minutes, but don't discard the roasting juices.

4 Cover the lamb with the mustard and garnish with the diced chives – they'll stick to the Dijon. Give it a drizzle of olive oil and serve the roasting juices separately.

Roast rump of lamb with olives, olive oil and roasting juices

Serves 2–3

2 tablespoons stoned
   black olives
Rump of lamb, about 350g
Extra virgin olive oil
   (or clarified butter)
Fresh herbs of your
   choice, to garnish

1 Preheat the oven to 180°C/gas 4.
2 Slice the olives and gently mash them, then set aside. Heat the olive oil or butter in a non-stick pan and caramelise the lamb on both sides. Transfer the lamb to a roasting tin, skin-side down, place it in the oven to roast for 10–15 minutes.
3 Remove the lamb from the oven and allow it to rest in a warm part of the kitchen for 5–10 minutes.
4 Spoon the mashed olives over the lamb and drizzle with olive oil before serving.

Roast rump of lamb with clams and roasting juices

Serves 2–3

1 tablespoon extra virgin
    olive oil (or clarified butter)
Rump of lamb, about 350g
A splash of white wine
2 bay leaves, to garnish
1 sprig of fresh thyme,
    to garnish
About 150g clams

1 Preheat the oven to 180°C/gas 4.
2 Heat olive oil or butter in a non-stick frying pan and caramelise the lamb on both sides. Transfer the lamb to a roasting tin, skin-side down, place in the oven and roast for 10–15 minutes.
3 Remove the lamb from the oven and allow the meat to rest for 5–10 minutes, but don't discard the roasting juices.
4 Heat a saucepan and pour in the white wine, bay leaves and thyme. Add the clams to the pan, cover with a lid and let them steam for a minute. Lift the lid, splash olive oil over the clams, cover again and shake the pan. Discard any clams that do not open.
5 Pour the roasting juices over the lamb, add the clams and garnish the meat with the thyme and bay leaves.

Roast rump of lamb with wild mushrooms and roasting juices

Serves 2–3

1 Preheat the oven to 180°C/gas 4.

2 Heat the olive oil or butter in a non-stick frying pan and caramelise the lamb on both sides. Transfer the lamb to a roasting tin, skin-side down, place in the oven and roast for 10–15 minutes.

3 Remove the lamb from the oven and allow the meat to rest for 5–10 minutes, but don't discard the roasting juices.

4 Meanwhile, boil the Madeira in a saucepan until it has evaporated and reduced to almost a syrup. Combine the roasting juices with the Madeira reduction.

5 In a pan, fry the mushrooms in olive oil over a medium heat for a minute or until they are cooked to your taste.

6 To serve, slice the lamb and spoon the mushrooms over and around the meat. Pour over the syrupy juices and scatter with fresh herbs.

Extra virgin olive oil
    (or clarified butter)
Rump of lamb, about 350g
100ml Madeira
150g wild mushrooms
Fresh herbs of your
    choice, to garnish

Roast rump of lamb with mint vinaigrette and roasting juices

Serves 2–3

Extra virgin olive oil
  (or clarified butter)
Rump of lamb, about 350g
2 teaspoons white wine
  vinegar
10g caster sugar
6 fresh mint leaves,
  finely chopped
2 shallots, diced, to serve
Fresh herbs of your
  choice, to garnish

1 Preheat the oven to 180°C/gas 4.
2 Heat olive oil or butter in a pan and caramelise the lamb on both sides. Transfer the lamb to a roasting tin, skin-side down, place in the oven and roast for 10–15 minutes.
3 Remove the lamb from the oven and allow the meat to rest for 5–10 minutes, but don't discard the roasting juices.
4 In a saucepan, combine the vinegar and sugar and bring to the boil. Add the roasting juices and the chopped mint leaves and continue to heat for a minute or two, so that the flavours meet and mix well.
5 Slice the lamb and pour over the vinaigrette and serve it with a sprinkling of diced shallots and fresh herbs.

Double pork chops roasted with Dijon mustard, dill cucumber and chives

Serves 2

1 double pork chop (2 chops joined, ask your butcher to remove the chine bone and skin, but to leave a layer of fat)

Clarified butter (or extra virgin olive oil)

1 small, sweet dill cucumber

Dijon mustard, to your taste

Fresh chives, finely snipped

Fresh flat-leaf parsley leaves (or fresh herbs of your choice), to garnish

1 Preheat the oven to 160°C/gas 2–3.

2 First brown the chops, skin-side down, for a few minutes in a hot pan of butter. Transfer the chops to an ovenproof dish and roast for 30–40 minutes. Remove the chops from the oven and let the meat rest for 10 minutes in a warm part of the kitchen.

3 Meanwhile, finely slice the dill cucumber, lengthways, then cut into dice.

4 Cover the pork with Dijon mustard and then coat it with the diced dill and chives; they will stick to the mustard. Garnish with parsley before serving.

Double pork chops roasted with black pepper and mangos

Serves 2

1 double pork chop (2 chops
  joined, ask your butcher
  to remove the chine bone
  and skin, but to leave a
  layer of fat)
Clarified butter (or
  extra virgin olive oil)
Extra virgin olive oil
2 whole star anise
2 large slices of mango,
  skin on
Fresh coriander, to garnish

For the honey glaze
100ml honey
10ml vinegar
10ml dark soy sauce
Freshly ground black pepper

1 Preheat the oven to 160°C/gas 2–3.
2 First brown the chops, skin-side down, for a few minutes in a hot pan of butter. Transfer the chops to an ovenproof dish and roast for 30–40 minutes. Remove the chops from the oven and let the meat rest for 10 minutes in a warm part of the kitchen.
3 Meanwhile, in a saucepan, mix the glaze ingredients together and bring to the boil.
4 In a separate pan, heat a teaspoon of olive oil and add the star anise and mango slices. Fry until the mango is golden brown.
5 When it comes to serving, slice the double chop in half and spoon over the hot glaze, letting the juices of the meat mix with the sweetness of the glaze. Place a star anise on each chop, put the caramelised mango onto the plate and scatter over fresh coriander.

Double pork chops roasted with prunes and bacon

Serves 2

1 double pork chop (2 chops joined; ask your butcher to remove the chine bone and skin, but to leave a layer of fat)
Clarified butter (or extra virgin olive oil)
100ml port
100ml prune juice
1 dessertspoon double cream
1 teaspoon Knorr concentrated chicken stock
About 50g bacon lardons
6 prunes

1 Preheat the oven to 160°C/gas 2–3.
2 First brown the chops, skin-side down for a few minutes in a hot pan of butter. Transfer the chops to an ovenproof dish and roast for 30–40 minutes. Remove the chops from the oven and let the meat rest for 10 minutes in a warm part of the kitchen.
3 Meanwhile, in a saucepan, boil the port until it has thickened, evaporated and reduced right down to about a teaspoon of syrup. Add the prune juice, cream and chicken stock. Continue to boil for a few minutes, until the sauce has reduced by about half (or to a consistency to your taste).
4 In a separate pan, fry the bacon and prunes in the remaining butter. Take a spoonful of the fat from the lardons and add it to the sauce.
5 Carve the double chops into two, pour over the sauce and garnish with the prunes and bacon.

Double pork chops roasted with apples, sage and cider cream sauce

Serves 2

1 double pork chop (2 chops joined; ask your butcher to remove the chine bone and skin, but to leave a layer of fat)

Clarified butter (or extra virgin olive oil)

A knob of unsalted butter

2 generous pinches of caster sugar

1 dessert apple, unpeeled, uncored and cut into thick segments

100ml cider

100ml apple juice

100ml double cream

1 teaspoon Knorr concentrated chicken stock

A splash of Calvados (optional)

Sage leaves, to garnish

1 Preheat the oven to 160°C/gas 2–3.

2 First brown the chops, skin-side down, for a few minutes in a hot pan of butter. Transfer the chops to an ovenproof dish and roast for 30–40 minutes. Remove the chops from the oven and let the meat rest for 10 minutes in a warm part of the kitchen.

3 Meanwhile, melt the butter and sugar in a pan, add the apple segments, skin-side up, and caramelise the apple.

4 To make the sauce, first boil the cider in a saucepan until it is reduced in volume to about a teaspoon of syrup. Now add the apple juice and continue to boil for a minute or so until it is again reduced to almost a syrup. Remove the pan from the heat and pour in the cream and the chicken stock. Return the pan to the heat and bring to the boil. (If you wish, add a splash of Calvados at this stage.)

5 Arrange the chops and caramelised apple on plates. Put the sage leaves on top of the chops and spoon over the sauce.

Double pork chops roasted with morels, Madeira and cream

Serves 2

1 Preheat the oven to 160°C/gas 2–3.
2 First brown the chops, skin-side down for a few minutes in a hot pan of butter. Transfer the chops to an ovenproof dish and roast for 30–40 minutes. Remove the chops from the oven and let the meat rest for 10 minutes in a warm part of the kitchen.
3 Meanwhile, in a saucepan, rapidly boil the Madeira until it is reduced in volume to about a teaspoon of syrup. Stir in the cream and chicken stock, and taste. Reduce to a low heat to keep the sauce warm.
4 In another pan, fry the morels in butter for 2 minutes before draining them in a colander to remove any excess butter. Return them to the pan and combine with the Madeira sauce before serving with the chops. Scatter with fresh herbs.

1 double pork chop (2 chops joined; ask your butcher to remove the chine bone and skin, but to leave a layer of fat)
Clarified butter (or extra virgin olive oil)
100ml Madeira
50ml double cream
1 teaspoon Knorr concentrated chicken stock
100g morels
A knob of unsalted butter
Fresh herbs of your choice, to garnish

Double pork chops roasted with apples and a Marco Polo glaze

Serves 2

1 double pork chop (2 chops joined, ask your butcher to remove the chine bone and skin, but to leave a layer of fat)

Clarified butter (or extra virgin olive oil)

50ml honey

1 teaspoon coriander seeds

2 whole star anise

10ml water

Fresh herbs of your choice, to garnish

1 Preheat the oven to 160°C/gas 2–3.

2 First brown the chops, skin-side down, for a few minutes in a hot pan of melted butter. Transfer the chops to an ovenproof dish and roast for 30–40 minutes. Remove the chops from the oven and let the meat rest for 10 minutes in a warm part of the kitchen.

3 To make the glaze, in a saucepan combine the honey, coriander seeds and star anise with the water in a saucepan. Bring to the boil and cook until it has thickened to your taste. Remove from the heat and stir in the juices from the ovenproof dish.

4 Slice the chop in two. Serve with a star anise on each chop and glaze before serving. Scatter with fresh herbs.

A joint of calf's liver, coated in black pepper, roasted in the oven for about 15 minutes, and served with raisins flamed in Armagnac

Serves 6

About 800g calf's liver
 (or whole liver)
Enough finely crushed
 black peppercorns to
 coat the liver
Clarified butter (or ghee
 or extra virgin olive oil)
A handful of raisins or
 currants
A generous splash of
 Armagnac
Fresh herbs of your choice,
 to garnish

1 Preheat the oven to 190°C/gas 5.
2 Dust one side of the liver with the pepper. In a large frying pan, heat the butter and fry the liver, pepper-side down, for 2 minutes. Turn the liver over, so it is now pepper-side up, and transfer it to an ovenproof dish to roast for 12–15 minutes. Remove from the oven and leave to rest in a warm place in the kitchen for a good 10 minutes.
3 Meanwhile, fry the raisins in butter for a minute or so and then pour in a generous splash of Armagnac. It will flame – be careful not to singe your hair.
4 Slice the liver and spoon the raisins, along with their Armagnac-infused butter, over the liver and serve scattered with fresh herbs.

Roasted joint of calf's liver with Dijon mustard and chives

Serves 6

1 Preheat the oven to 190°C/gas 5.
2 In a large frying pan, heat the butter and fry the liver for a couple of minutes, then turn the liver and transfer it to an ovenproof dish to roast for 12–15 minutes. Remove from the oven and leave to rest in a warm place in the kitchen for a good 10 minutes.
3 When the liver is cool enough to handle, spread the mustard over and then roll it in the chives (they'll stick to the mustard). Serve with fresh herbs.

By the way…You could do the same with lamb's liver, again starting it off in the pan before roasting it for about 5 to 8 minutes in the oven.

About 800g calf's liver (or whole liver)
Clarified butter (or ghee or extra virgin olive oil)
Dijon mustard, to your taste
2 handfuls of chives, finely diced
Fresh herbs of your choice, to garnish

Four more ways with liver

Serves 3–6

6 slices of calf's liver
3 tablespoons breadcrumbs
clarified butter (or extra virgin olive oil)

Add the slices of liver to a heavy-based frying pan and fry in foaming butter for a minute on each side. Remove from the heat and let the liver continue to cook in the gentle heat of the pan.

in parsley breadcrumbs
Top left

3 tablespoons parsley, finely chopped

1 Mix the parsley with the breadcrumbs and toss the slices of liver in the mixture until coated.
2 In a large frying pan, melt the butter to a hazelnut brown. Fry the slices of liver for a minute on one side, then turn over and cook for 10 seconds. Remove the pan from the heat and let the liver continue to cook in the gentle heat of the pan for a couple of minutes before serving.

in sage breadcrumbs
Bottom left

½ heaped tablespoons fresh sage, finely chopped

1 Mix the sage with the breadcrumbs and then toss the liver in the mixture until coated.
2 Fry the liver as before.
3 If you wish, garnish with sage leaves. They aren't palatable unless cooked, so try this technique: stretch clingfilm across a plate to make a drum and, using a pastry brush, paint the drum with a teaspoon of olive oil. Lay 6 sage leaves out and then cover with another layer of clingfilm. Microwave for 2–2½ minutes. This will also work with basil leaves.

with bacon and sage
Top right

6 fresh sage leaves
6 rashers good quality bacon, halved

1 Fry the liver as before and grill the bacon until cooked to your liking.
2 Put 2 slices of bacon on each slice of liver along with a sage leaf. Pour over the sage butter from the pan and serve. Simple and very Italian.

with devils on horseback
Bottom right

Tabasco sauce, to your taste
60g mango chutney
6 rashers good quality streaky bacon
6 Agen prunes, stoned
Plain flour

1 Make the devils: add the Tabasco to the mango chutney; spoon a dollop of the chutney-Tabasco mixture and a prune on to each bacon rasher; roll up tight. Grill, turning once or twice, until the bacon has caramelised.
2 Dust the liver in flour and fry as before. Leave the liver in the pan and allow it to continue cooking in gentle heat. Serve with the devils.

Liver and onions

Serves 1

1 onion, halved and
  finely sliced
A generous amount of
  clarified butter (or
  unsalted butter or ghee)
1 piece of liver
Fresh herbs of your choice,
  to garnish

1 Fry the onion in a generous amount of foaming butter for about 5 minutes, or until it is golden and crisp (but don't burn it). Drain the onion but keep the butter.

2 Fry the liver in the butter. Top the liver with the onions and a scattering of fresh herbs.

Devilled kidneys

Serves 3–4

600g lamb or veal kidneys,
  sliced into chunks
Extra virgin olive oil
Hot toast, to serve

For the sauce
375ml HP sauce
285ml Lea & Perrins
  Worcestershire sauce
60ml Tabasco sauce
125ml sherry
1 tablespoon caster sugar
50g unsalted butter

*For the flour mixture
  for the kidneys*
6 tablespoons plain flour
2 tablespoons cayenne
  pepper
2 tablespoons mustard
  powder

1 In a saucepan mix the sauce ingredients, except
the butter, and cook but don't bring to the boil.
Add the butter and let it melt, then remove the
pan from the heat and set aside.
2 Combine the ingredients for the flour mixture in
a shallow bowl. Dust the kidneys in the flour mixture
and then brown them in a frying pan with olive oil,
turning once or twice. Add the cooked kidneys to
the sauce. Stir and serve on hot toast.

Turkey is the king of poultry. Forget the overcooked stuff that's dry. It has to be cooked well and then it's delicious, as I've been saying for years.

As for chicken? I was once asked what I'd have for my last meal. Roast chicken, I replied. Thighs or breast? Drumsticks, actually. They're the tastiest part of the bird, I reckon, and that's why I use them in the Knorr stockpot.

Poultry

★ ★ ★

Roast chicken with Merlot vinegar

Serves 4

1 chicken, about 1.2kg
5 tablespoons extra virgin
  olive oil
100ml Merlot vinegar
1 shallot, finely chopped
Fresh herbs of your choice,
  to garnish

1 Preheat the oven to 180°C/gas 4.
2 Put the chicken in a large roasting tin and pour over the olive oil. You want the oil to coat the skin of the bird.
3 Roast the chicken in the oven for about 40–50 minutes, basting it a couple of times during cooking, until the chicken is tender.
4 When cooked, remove the chicken from the roasting tin and leave until it is cool to the touch. Reserve all the juices and olive oil that remain in the roasting tin.
5 Boil the vinegar in a frying pan until it has evaporated and reduced in volume by about half. Keep tasting: it will sweeten, thicken and become softer on the palate – and then it will be syrupy.
6 To make the sauce, combine the cooled juices and oil from the roasting tin with the reduced vinegar in the frying pan – give it just a gentle stir so that the liquids are not fully mixed. Carve the chicken, scatter over the chopped shallot and pour over the sauce and add a sprinkling of fresh herbs.

By the way… Often you will be advised to check that roast chicken is cooked by inserting a skewer into the thickest part of the meat to see if the juices run clear. However, when the bird is resting it will continue to cook (albeit at a lower temperature) so take that into consideration – in other words, don't overcook it. If you don't have Merlot vinegar to hand, then why not try a different vinegar; white wine vinegar works well.

Roast chicken ketchup with fresh herbs

Serves 4

1 Preheat the oven to 180°C/gas 4.

2 Put the chicken in a large roasting tin and pour over the olive oil, so that it's nicely coated. Roast the chicken in the oven for 40–50 minutes, basting the bird once or twice, until the chicken is tender.

3 Meanwhile, make the sauce by mixing all the ingredients together.

4 Remove the chicken from the oven and leave until it is cool enough to touch. Carve the chicken and spoon the sauce over the meat. Scatter over some chopped herbs, such as tarragon, basil, parsley or chives, and serve or have it cold and make it the star of a picnic on a hot day.

1 chicken, about 1.2kg
50ml extra virgin olive oil
Fresh herbs of your choice, to garnish

For the ketchup sauce
170g tomato ketchup
50g shallots, finely chopped
1 tablespoon fresh chives, finely chopped
1 tablespoon fresh tarragon, finely chopped
1 tablespoon fresh chervil, finely chopped
2 tablespoons Lea & Perrins Worcestershire sauce
About 10 drops Tabasco sauce, or to your taste
2 tablespoons white wine vinegar
Maldon sea salt
150ml extra virgin olive oil

Chicken with Knorr and parsley gravy

Serves 4

1 chicken, about 1.2kg
5 dessertspoons extra virgin
   olive oil
200ml water
1½ tablespoons Knorr
   concentrated chicken stock
A handful of fresh flat-leaf
   parsley (or fresh herbs of
   your choice), to garnish

1 Preheat the oven to 180°C/gas 4.

2 Put the chicken in a large roasting tin and pour over the olive oil. You want to coat the skin of the bird.

3 Roast the chicken for about 40–50 minutes, basting it a couple of times during cooking, until the chicken is tender.

4 When cooked, remove the chicken from the roasting tin and leave until it is cool to the touch. Reserve the juices and olive oil that remain in the roasting tin.

5 The sauce won't take long to make. First, combine the water and chicken stock in a frying pan (along with bits of wings and carcass) and bring to the boil. Cook for 3–4 minutes – notice how the taste of the sauce develops and intensifies.

6 Combine this mixture with the cooled juices and oil from the roasting tin – give it just a gentle stir so that the liquids are not fully mixed. Carve the chicken, pour over the sauce and scatter over the parsley or other fresh herbs.

154

Roast chicken with wild mushrooms and Madeira flavoured roasting juices

Serves 4

1 chicken, about 1.2kg
5 dessertspoons extra virgin olive oil
A generous amount of wild mushrooms (I like girolle)
Clarified butter
150ml Madeira (or port)
Fresh herbs of your choice, to garnish

1 Preheat the oven to 180°C/gas 4.

2 Put the chicken in a large roasting tin and pour over the olive oil. You want it to coat the skin of the bird.

3 Roast the chicken for about 40–50 minutes, basting it a couple of times during cooking, until the chicken is cooked and tender.

4 When cooked, remove the chicken from the roasting tin and leave until it is cool to the touch. Reserve the juices and olive oil that remain in the roasting tin.

5 While the chicken is resting, slice the mushrooms and fry them in some butter for about 1 minute, then remove and set aside. In the same pan, add the Madeira and bring to the boil. Boil until it has evaporated, become syrupy and reduced in volume by about two-thirds. Keep tasting it and notice how its flavours intensify.

6 To make the sauce, combine the Madeira syrup with the cooled juices and oil from the roasting tin in the frying pan – give it just a gentle stir so that the liquids are not fully mixed. Carve the chicken, pour over the sauce and spoon over the wild mushrooms. Serve with the fresh herbs.

By the way… I have used girolle, but use the wild mushrooms that you prefer.

Chicken stockpot

Serves 4

1 Put the chicken drumsticks, carrots, onions, celery and stock cubes into a casserole dish or large, heavy-based saucepan and cover with cold water.
2 Cook on the hob for 1 hour or until the chicken is tender. Keep an eye on the heat; the water should simmer and not boil rapidly.
3 After an hour, remove the casserole or pan from the heat, add a splash of olive oil and stir in the thyme and bay leaf. Serve from the casserole, allowing 3 drumsticks per serving.

By the way...I cook the stockpot on top of the hob to reduce it quickly. If you prefer, cook it in the oven at about 180°C/gas 4.

12 large chicken drumsticks
6 medium-sized carrots, coarsely sliced
2 onions, finely sliced
1 celery stick, coarsely sliced
3 Knorr chicken stock cubes
Extra virgin olive oil
2 sprigs of fresh thyme
1 bay leaf

Turkey thigh stuffed on the bone, with gravy

Serves 4

1 small packet (85g) Paxo
   sage and onion stuffing
1 turkey thigh, about 600g
100ml water
A pinch of Knorr chicken
   stock cube
1 tablespoon milk
½ teaspoon cornflour
Maldon sea salt and freshly
   ground pepper
Fresh herbs of your choice,
   to garnish

1 Preheat the oven to 180°C/gas 4.

2 Make the Paxo stuffing and insert it inside the turkey thigh, around the bone. Place in a roasting tin and roast for 70–80 minutes, remove from the oven and allow to rest in a warm part of the kitchen for at least 10 minutes.

3 While the bird rests, make the gravy. Spoon off the excess fat from the roasting tin and then combine the roasting juices with the water. Bring to the boil, and add the pinch of stock cube.

4 Mix the milk with the cornflour to make a paste before adding a tablespoon of the boiling gravy to the paste. Combine, then pour the cornflour mixture into the gravy to thicken it. Taste and season if necessary.

5 Carve the turkey, serve with the piping hot gravy, and fresh herbs and think how Christmas can come every day.

Turkey steak with rosemary and Gruyère

Serves 2

1 Preheat the oven to 180°C/gas 4.
2 In a saucepan, bring the cream to the boil, then throw in the breadcrumbs, flour and cheese. Warm the sauce so that the cheese semi-melts, but keep it a little lumpy and then blitz it. Season with Worcestershire sauce. Add the egg yolk and rosemary and blend again – it should be like a ball of pasta dough. Chill in a bowl in the fridge.
3 Place the turkey steaks on a roasting tin and mould the paste on top of the turkey steak to the thickness you require. Roast in the oven for 10–12 minutes. Serve with some rosemary and fresh herbs.

30ml double cream
1 tablespoon natural white breadcrumbs
1 tablespoon plain flour
230g Gruyère cheese, grated
Lea & Perrins Worcestershire sauce, to your taste
1 egg yolk
2 turkey steaks (or fillets), about 150g each
Fresh rosemary leaves, chopped, to your taste
Fresh herbs of your choice, to garnish

163

Four more ways with turkey

Serves 2–3

2 turkey steaks or fillets, each weighing about 150g

After making the crusts, there are 2 simple steps:
1 Chill the crust mixture in the fridge and mould
on top of the turkey to the thickness that you like.
2 Roast for 10–12 minutes in a preheated oven at 180°C/gas 4
and then let the meat rest.

with a wild mushroom crust

Top left

100ml Madeira
½ teaspoon Knorr concentrated chicken stock
Clarified butter
100g white breadcrumbs
30g porcini powder
60g Gruyére cheese, grated
130g unsalted butter, softened

1 To make the crust, blend the breadcrumbs,
porcini powder and grated Gruyére. Add the
butter and blend again until it looks like a
ball of pasta dough.
2 Cook the turkey as before, but remember
to retain the juices.
3 To make the sauce, boil the Madeira until it is
reduced to almost a syrup. Add the chicken stock
and the clarified butter and cook for a minute.
Remove the pan from the heat and stir in the
roasting juices before pouring over the turkey.

with a sage and onion crust

Bottom left

2 bacon rashers, halved
30g Paxo sage and onion stuffing
A knob of unsalted butter

1 Make up the stuffing mix and spread it on
top of the steak.
2 Lay the bacon rashers on top of the stuffing
and roast for 10–12 minutes with a knob of butter.

with a Welsh rarebit crust

Top right

30ml double cream
1 tablespoon white breadcrumbs
1 tablespoon plain flour
½ tablespoon mustard powder
230g Cheddar cheese, grated
Lea & Perrins Worcestershire sauce, to your taste
1 egg yolk

1 Bring the cream to the boil, then throw in the
breadcrumbs, flour, mustard powder and cheese.
Warm the sauce until it's in little lumps but don't
melt the cheese fully, and then blend. Season with
Worcestershire sauce and add the egg yolk.
2 Cook the turkey as before.

with a walnut crust

Bottom right

100ml Madeira
½ teaspoon Knorr concentrated chicken stock
Walnut oil, to your taste
Clarified butter
60g walnuts, crushed
60g white breadcrumbs
130g unsalted butter, softened
60g Gruyére cheese, grated

1 To make the crust, blend the walnuts and
breadcrumbs. Add the butter and Gruyére and
blend until it looks like a ball of pasta dough.
2 Follow steps 1-2, above, retaining the juices again.
3 To make the sauce, boil the Madeira as before,
also adding walnut oil.
4 Carry to the table whistling Ding, Dong,
Merrily on High.

What do I dream of? I had a dream that I was puréeing bananas and mixing them with custard. The next thing I knew I was awake and eager to make what I call Jamaican mess, the dish inspired by my strange dream. It's delicious.

When I was a kid, Sunday lunch was often tinned fruit with condensed milk, made by Carnation, of course. Fruit salads and fruit poached in wine, which are great, easy-to-make dishes that can be carried to the table in large bowls. Remember, a sense of sensation is what it's all about. And nowadays Carnation make a caramel sauce — perfect for the mess dishes.

Desserts

Rhubarb burnt cream

Serves 6

400g rhubarb
150g caster sugar
1 tablespoon water

For the burnt cream mix
900ml double cream
100ml whole milk
2 vanilla pods, halved
    and sliced lengthways
9 egg yolks
150g caster sugar, plus
    extra for topping

1 Preheat the oven to 170°C/gas 3.

2 Finely slice the rhubarb and then put in an ovenproof dish with the sugar and mix together. Add the water and cook in the oven for 20 minutes, until the rhubarb has softened.

3 Remove from the oven and drain away the liquid. Using a stick blender, turn the sugary cooked rhubarb into a purée. Now put the purée back into the ovenproof dish (the brulée mix will be poured over it). Reduce the oven temperature to 95°C/gas ¼ .

4 In a separate saucepan combine the cream, milk and vanilla pods and bring to the boil. Meanwhile, in a bowl, whisk together the egg yolks and sugar for a few seconds so they are fully mixed.

5 Pour the boiling cream-milk mixture over the eggs and continue to whisk so that you don't end up with scrambled eggs. Remove the vanilla pods and scrape the seeds into the mixture.

6 Pour the mixture into the ovenproof dish and cook in the oven for 35 minutes.

7 When cooked, remove the dish from the oven and allow to cool. Sprinkle half the sugar over the cream and brown the sugar and make it crunchy, preferably with a kitchen blowtorch, or failing that, by putting it under a hot grill.

8 Leave the caramel topping to cool and then sprinkle over the remaining sugar and repeat the browning process. It should be served immediately.

Four ways with messes

Serves 4

500ml double cream
1 ½ teaspoon vanilla extract
50g icing sugar
4 meringue nests, broken up
1 pot Ambrosia custard (135g)

Combine the cream, icing sugar and vanilla extract and whip the mixture to a thin ribbon consistency, being careful not to over-whisk. Fold in the broken meringue.

Jamaican mess

Top left

2 bananas, broken down with a fork
2 dessertspoons Carnation
    caramel sauce

Create the meringue mixture and fold in the bananas, the custard and the caramel. Serve.

Eton mess

Top right

50g icing sugar
500g strawberries, crushed with
    a sprinkling of icing sugar

Create the meringue mixture as before, and fold in the raspberries and strawberries.

Rhubarb and custard mess

Bottom left

600g rhubarb, finely sliced
50g caster sugar

1 Combine the rhubarb and sugar. Place tinfoil over the top of the dish, and bake in an oven pre-heated to 170C for 25 minutes until the fruit is soft. Drain off the liquid and blitz half of the cooked rhubarb to a purée. Leave to cool.
2 Fold in the rhubarb purée and garnish with the remaining half of the rhubarb.

Mango and ginger mess

Bottom right

600g fresh mango
Fresh ginger, cut lengthways
    into matchsticks
2 dessertspoons Carnation
    caramel sauce
150g caster sugar
150ml water

1 Using a stick blender, blitz the mango to a purée. Blanch the ginger in boiling water for 10 seconds. Remove, drain and refresh under cold water for a few seconds. Repeat this process two more times to remove the bitterness.
2 Make s stock syrup in a saucepan by combining the water and the caster sugar, throw in the ginger and bring to the boil. Cook for a couple of minutes until the ginger is nicely tender.
3 Create the meringue mixture as before and fold in the mango purée, ginger matchsticks, custard and caramel, and serve.

Peaches poached in Champagne

Serves 6

1 bottle Champagne
  (or Prosecco)
600g caster sugar
6 peaches

1 In a casserole or ovenproof dish combine the Champagne and sugar. Bring to the boil and stir so that the sugar dissolves.

2 Put the peaches into the liquid and put an upturned plate on top of them to keep them submerged in the liquid. Turn down the heat and simmer gently for about 10 minutes, or until the tip of a knife can penetrate the peach without resistance.

3 Remove from the heat and allow the fruit to cool in its own syrup. Serve with a little crème fraîche.

Peaches in Sauternes Jelly

Serves 6

6 peaches
400g sugar
1 litre Sauternes
6 leaves gelatine

1 In a casserole or ovenproof dish combine the Sauternes and sugar and bring to the boil, stirring so that the sugar dissolves. Put the peaches into the liquid and put an upturned plate on top of them to keep them submerged.

2 Turn down the heat and simmer gently for about 10 minutes, or until the tip of a knife can penetrate the peach without resistance. Remove from the liquid and set aside to cool.

3 Add gelatine to two-thirds of the liquid following the instructions on the packet. Be sure to arrange the fruit so that you can serve easily, with enough space to fit a serving spoon in between each peach. Serve the remaining third of the liquid as a syrup to pour over the jelly.

By the way…Sauternes is quite pricey. You could use a less expensive dessert wine, in which case use 600mg of sugar to 1 litre wine.

Pears poached in red wine and spices

Serves 6

1 Blanch the pears in boiling water for 30 seconds and then peel and remove the cores, but leave on the stalks. Pour the wine and sugar into a large casserole or ovenproof dish and add the star anise, cloves and cinnamon sticks. Bring to the boil and give a good stir to ensure no sugar is stuck to the bottom of the pan.
2 Put the pears into the dish and put an upturned plate on top of the pears to keep them submerged.
3 Cover the dish with clingfilm, bring to the boil and then reduce the heat to a gentle simmer so you don't spoil the beautiful pears. Simmer gently for about 10 minutes, or until the tip of a knife can penetrate the pear flesh without resistance. Allow the fruit to cool in the syrup and serve from the dish at the table.

6 pears
2 bottles red wine
3 star anise
5 cloves
2 cinnamon sticks
1kg caster sugar

Pears poached with Vanilla

Serves 6

1 Peel the pears and remove the cores, but leave on the stalks. Pour the wine and sugar into a large casserole or ovenproof dish and add the vanilla. Bring to the boil and stir the wine mixture to ensure sugar isn't stuck to the bottom of the pan.
2 Put the pears into the dish and put an upturned plate on top of the pears to keep them submerged.
3 Cover the dish with clingfilm, bring to the boil and then reduce the heat to a really gentle simmer. Simmer for about 10 minutes, or until the tip of a knife can penetrate the pear flesh without resistance. Allow the fruit to cool in the syrup and serve from the dish at the table.

By the way...Why not try apricots with vanilla, following the recipe as above but swapping pears for apricots.

6 pears
2 bottles white wine
450g caster sugar
1–2 vanilla pods, sliced
lengthways in half

Lemon syllabub

Serves 4

For the lemon syrup
80g caster sugar
Juice of 3 lemons
40ml water

2 lemons
30g icing sugar
500ml double cream
3 tablespoons
  Limoncello liqueur

1 In a saucepan make the syrup by combining the caster sugar with the water and bring to the boil. Just before it starts to colour, add the lemon juice. Boil for a few minutes until it has thickened and remove from the heat (remember, the syrup will be a lot thicker when it cools).
2 Peel the lemon so that you end up with long matchsticks of lemon zest and then, with a sharp knife, slice away the pith. Blanch the zest by putting it into a saucepan of water, bring to the boil, count to 10 and remove from the heat. Refresh the zest by draining it in a colander and immediately running it under cold water for a few seconds. Repeat this process twice.
3 Making the syllabub will take just a minute or two. Combine the icing sugar and cream and whip to a thick ribbon consistency, being careful not to over-whisk (unless you want to end up with cheese). Fold in the strips of lemon and chilled lemon syrup and finish by drizzling over the Limoncello.

By the way...Syllabub is the first dessert I ever made as a chef. No one knows quite where the name comes from. At the hotel St. George in the Yorkshire town of Harrogate we used to make it with sweet white wine, as was the tendancy in those days. And Limoncello, the lemon liqueur, takes me straight back to my Italian roots.

Tropical fruit salad with passion fruit syrup

Serves 6–8

Tropical fruit of
  your choice but
  could include:
1 pineapple
3 bananas
2 mangos
2 kiwi fruits

For the syrup
800g passion fruit
200ml orange juice
400g caster sugar

1 First make the syrup. Remove the seeds and pith from the passion fruit. Blend the passion fruit almost to a pulp. Using a spoon, and in a saucepan, combine it with the orange juice and sugar and bring it to the boil. Continue to cook for about 5 minutes or until it thickens and becomes syrupy. Allow to cool.
2 Slice the fruit into large chunks. Arrange carefully, building up the salad with your fingers. Do not toss it with spoons. Pour the syrup over the fruit and serve.

Red fruit salad in red wine syrup

Serves 6

1 First make the syrup. In a saucepan, combine the red wine and caster sugar, bring to the boil and stir to ensure the sugar dissolves.
2 Arrange the fruit carefully in a serving bowl; don't cut the strawberries. Pour the red wine syrup over the fruit and serve.

Use the red fruit you
   like or you could try:
250g raspberries
250g strawberries
   (the smaller the better)
250g fraises des bois
   or wild strawberries

For the syrup
½ bottle red wine
300g caster sugar

Fresh raspberries in rosé wine jelly

Serves 4–6

750g raspberries
1½ bottles rosé wine
750g caster sugar
10 leaves gelatine

1 Soak the gelatine in very cold water. This will soften it, making it easily dissolvable.
2 Arrange the raspberries in a shallow dish.
3 In a saucepan, combine the wine and sugar and bring to the boil, stirring to help the sugar dissolve. Remove from the heat and allow to cool.
4 Keep some of the syrup to pour over the jelly. Make the jelly by adding gelatine to the remaining liquid, following the instructions on the gelatine packet or using 10 leaves, as suggested.
5 Layer the raspberries, adding a little of the jelly each time and then returning it to the fridge. This stops the raspberries from floating and produces a glorious layered jelly.

Cherries Jubilee

Serves 6

1kg cherries
100ml Kirsch
400ml water
250g caster sugar
Ice cream, to serve

1 Slice the cherries or remove the stones and leave whole – your choice.
2 In a saucepan, combine the Kirsch, water and sugar and bring to the boil to make a syrup. Pour the syrup over the cherries and serve immediately with ice cream.

By the way… This dish was created by Escoffier and traditionally the syrup was thickened with cornflour, but I prefer to keep it light, so leave out the flour.

Affogato

Serves 1

1½ dessertspoons Camp coffee (or to your taste)
240ml water
2–3 balls of vanilla ice cream

1 Mix the Camp coffee with the water and bring to the boil in a small saucepan.

2 Pour the boiling coffee over the ice cream. Affogato is Italian for drowned – so be generous when you pour.

3 Eat it immediately, while also considering that traditionally you'd need an expensive espresso machine to make this dish.

First published in Great Britain in 2010
by Weidenfeld & Nicolson

1 3 5 7 9 10 8 6 4 2

A CIP catalogue record for this book is available from the British Library.

ISBN 978 1 4072 3381 9

Designed by Smith & Gilmour
Printed and bound in China

The Orion Publishing Group's policy is to use papers that are natural,
renewable and recyclable and made from wood grown in sustainable
forests. The logging and manufacturing processes are expected to conform
to the environmental regulations of the country of origin.

Weidenfeld & Nicolson
The Orion Publishing Group Ltd
Orion House
5 Upper Saint Martin's Lane
London WC2H 9EA

An Hachette UK Company

www.orionbooks.co.uk